Love to Sew

Cakes & Candies

Dedication

To Mike Fitchett, my chief taster.

Love to Sew

Cakes & Candies

Greta Fitchett

Search Press

First published in Great Britain 2013

Search Press Limited
Wellwood, North Farm Road,
Tunbridge Wells, Kent TN2 3DR

Text copyright © Greta Fitchett 2013

Photographs by Paul Bricknell at Search Press studios

Photographs and design copyright © Search Press Ltd. 2013

ISBN: 978-1-84448-792-9

The Publishers and author can accept no responsibility for any consequences arising from the information, advice or instructions given in this publication.

Suppliers
If you have difficulty in obtaining any of the materials and equipment mentioned in this book, then please visit the Search Press website for details of suppliers:
www.searchpress.com

Acknowledgements

I wish to thank Mike Fitchett, for his practical help that makes so much possible; Laurence Kimpton, who bought the box of chocolates that sparked the original idea of making calorie-free edibles from fabric; Kathy Troup of *Stitch* magazine, who published the original box of chocolates pro[...]

Katie French a[...]

Printed in China

Sweet Romance, page 22

Golden Days, page 24

My Valentine, page 30

Pink Candies, page 32

Bedazzled, page 38

Lemon Bonbons, page 40

Meringues, page 50

Teatime Treats, page 52

Easter Treats, page 26

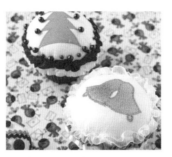

Festive Cakes, page 28

Contents

Jewelled Candies, page 34

Sugar Shimmers, page 36

Happy Birthday, page 42

Chocolate Box, page 44

Button Cakes, page 46

Pincushions, page 48

Fondant Fancies, page 54

Butterfly Cakes, page 56

Fruit Tarts, page 58

Cherry Turnover, page 60

Introduction

If you have watched your baking disappear quickly from the cooling rack, or if you worry about the calories the cakes contain, then this book will provide the answer – calorie-free cakes!

Here is a collection of small, mouth-watering sewing projects inspired by candies, chocolates, cakes and pies. The basic techniques are easy to master, and I've used a variety of fabrics, ribbons, buttons and beads to create a range of finishes, including piped cream, tasty fruits and delicious-looking toppings. Different colours are used to convey different flavours, and there are themed ideas for special events such as weddings, anniversaries, Mother's Day, Valentine's Day, and seasonal events such as Christmas and Easter.

The finished projects are surprisingly realistic and require only small quantities of materials, so they are ideal for using up off-cuts of fabric and the left-over contents of your sewing basket. Your friends and family will be delighted to receive a little hand-sewn cake or candy as a special gift, and you will be amazed how easily the designs in this book can be personalised simply by altering the fabrics, colours or embellishments used. So feel free to over-indulge and make your own guilt-free, sumptuous, sugary feast!

Safety note:
Children will love the colourful cakes and candies in this book, but the projects are not intended as toys. Sew on any buttons or beads securely if children are likely to come into contact with them, and make sure they are kept out of the reach of very young children.

Materials & equipment

The projects can all be made with basic sewing tools, and a sewing machine will speed up your sewing and give stronger seams. Colour plays an important part when choosing materials as it helps to convey the texture and flavour. Once stitched, each project uses toy stuffing to create the three-dimensional shapes, and these are then decorated with a range of easy-to-find items that will make the projects great fun to make.

Sewing machine

Stitching using a sewing machine is preferable to hand stitching as it will give you stronger seams. These will withstand firm stuffing and the project will keep its shape better. A quarter-inch seam foot will help to maintain accurate seam allowances.

Fabrics

Most of the cakes and candies are made using plain cotton fabric. I use dark brown to suggest chocolate, various pastel shades for fruit flavours, and cream colours for vanilla. Cream-coloured silk polyester makes good piped cream and meringues, and crystal sheer fabric adds lustre to the cake surface.

Threads

Use a machine sewing thread, either cotton or polyester, to construct the projects. The same threads can be used to hand stitch yo-yos, gather ribbon and stitch buttons and beads to the cakes and candies. Rayon machine embroidery thread and metallic machine embroidery thread are used for satin-stitch edges. For hand embroidery stitches use stranded cotton or coton à broder.

Ribbons and lace

Double-sided satin ribbon is used to decorate the cakes. Once gathered, this creates the effect of luscious, piped butter icing and is available in cream, white and pastel colours. Various types of lace can also be used to create pretty finishes.

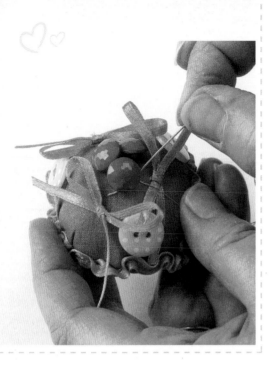

Beads and buttons

Small beads in various sizes are used to decorate the surfaces of the cakes and candies. Some can be used to make realistic-looking fruit decorations while others resemble sugar crystals and add a touch of sparkle to the finished piece. The smallest type I use are seed beads, and the largest are 4mm and 6mm pearl and crystal beads. Fun cakes suitable for children are decorated with buttons (there is plenty of choice in both colour and shape), but remember that the cakes are not playthings, and should not be given to young children.

Needles and pins

A hand-sewing needle is used to decorate the cakes, and an embroidery needle with a large eye is needed when using embroidery threads. Pearl beads can be sewn with a standard size needle, but finer beads such as seed beads require a beading needle. Pearl-headed pins can be used while constructing and decorating the cakes.

Cake cases

There is a huge range of cake cases available in many beautiful colours and designs. The chocolates and candies are displayed in petit four paper and foil cases. The small and large cupcakes are set in silicone cupcake cases that can be bought in bakeware shops and online in different colours. I've used two sizes: 3cm (1¼in) and 4cm (1½in) across the base.

Yo-yo makers

These tools are used to make a basic cake or candy shape. They are available in different sizes – I have used a 45mm (1¾in) diameter yo-yo maker for chocolates and candies, 60mm (2¼in) for small cupcakes, and 90mm (3½in) for large cupcakes. They make the projects quicker to make, but they are not essential, though if you are planning on making several projects it might be worth investing in two or three (they are not expensive to buy). Circular templates can be used to create the same effect.

Templates

Many of the projects in the book are based on a circle of fabric, the size of which varies depending on the type of cake or candy you are making. Other projects require templates to construct the basic cake shape, including butterfly cakes and pies. Appliquéd decorations also need a template. All of the templates are provided at the back of the book.

Other materials and equipment

I fill the stitched shapes using toy stuffing, which can be purchased from haberdashery shops, craft shops and online. Transfer adhesive is used for a quick-and-easy method of appliqué, and iron-on interfacing helps to stabilise the fabric while you are machine stitching. You will also need a pair of sharp scissors for cutting the fabric; a rotary cutter and cutting mat for cutting clean, straight lines; a pair of embroidery scissors for cutting the threads; and a tape measure, metal ruler, some safety pins and a thimble.

Basic techniques

These techniques are used for the projects in this book, and range from simple shapes based on circles of fabric to more complex constructions that require templates. There are also ideas for decorating the surface of the cakes and candies. If templates are required, these will need to be traced or photocopied on to paper or card and cut out ready for use.

Making a basic cake or candy shape

The least expensive way to create a basic cake or candy shape is by using circular paper templates; however, if you are planning on making several of the projects in this book you might prefer to invest in two or three yo-yo makers. Instructions for using both methods are provided here.

Using a circular paper template

1 Cut out a circle from a piece of paper and pin it to the fabric. Cut around the edge of the template.

2 Turn the edge of the fabric over by about 0.25cm (⅛in) and work small, even running stitches around the hem.

3 Pull the fabric into gathers and fasten off. The raw edge will turn inwards and there will be a small space at the centre for stuffing.

Using a yo-yo maker

This piece of equipment is easy to use; simply follow the manufacturer's instructions or the step-by-step instructions given below. The yo-yo maker is an accurate and quick way of making the basic cake and candy shapes. It holds the fabric firmly for cutting out and makes stitching easier and more regular. Use a thread colour that matches the fabric (though in the following demonstration, a different-coloured thread has been used for clarity).

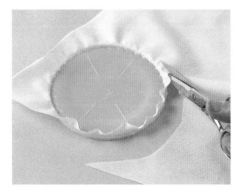

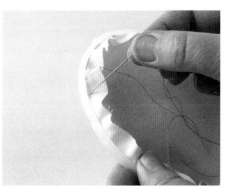

1 Lay the fabric on the tray part of the yo-yo maker, then lay the disk on top of this. Align the lines on the disk with the notches on the tray and clamp the two together. Trim off the excess fabric, leaving a 1cm (½in) border all round.

2 Thread a needle and make a starting knot in the thread. Stitch around the outer edge of the fabric. Fold the fabric over on to the disk part of the yo-yo maker as you work, and pass the needle through the holes in the tray.

3 Make sure that the stitches are lying in the gaps on the tray part of the yo-yo maker, otherwise you will be unable to release the fabric once stitching is complete.

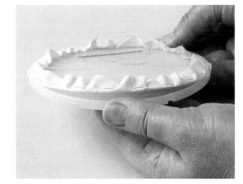

4 Stitch all the way around the yo-yo maker to just beyond the starting knot. With the thread on the top, push upwards through the hole in the centre of the tray and separate the two halves.

5 Separate the fabric from the disk part of the yo-yo maker, then pull up the thread to form gathers. When you have gathered the fabric sufficiently, fasten off the thread securely.

6 Carefully stuff the finished cake shape with toy stuffing. Use the points of a pair of fabric scissors to push in small clumps of the stuffing, and make sure the entire space is filled and firm with a smooth surface.

Making a thick, creamy, piped filling

To create this effect, gather a long tube of fabric using a sewing machine fitted with either a standard foot or an open-toe foot. The open-toe foot will allow you to see the line of stitching. Again, use a thread colour that matches the fabric rather than a contrasting thread – this is for clarity only in the demonstration below.

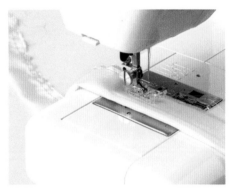

1 Cut a length of cream-coloured silk polyester about 8cm (3¼in) wide. Fold it in half lengthways, right sides together, and stitch along its length about 0.5cm (¼in) from the raw edge.

2 Turn the tube right side out by fastening a safety pin at one end and pushing it through to the other.

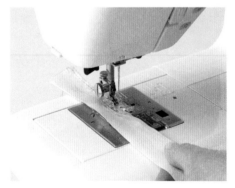

3 Roll the seam so that it is sitting at the edge of the fabric tube. Machine stitch along the seam, working close to the edge, using an extra-long stitch. Do not secure the threads at either end.

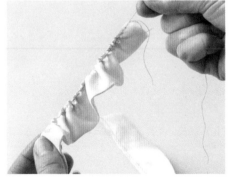

4 Pull one of the threads to draw the fabric tube into gathers and fasten off. For a slightly thicker cream filling, stuff the gathered tube lightly with a little toy stuffing.

Making a smooth cream filling

For a smooth cream filling, the fabric for the tube is cut on the bias, and the tube is either stuffed with toy filling or left unstuffed. If you are stuffing the tube, it should be no longer than about 38cm (15in) otherwise it will be difficult to stuff. Use scissors to pick up small amounts of stuffing and avoid overfilling the tube – it needs to be flexible enough to bend into the required shape.

  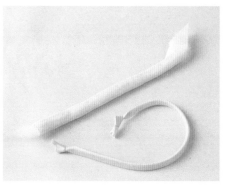

1 Fold a square of fabric diagonally on the bias, iron, then cut along the crease.

2 Cut a strip of fabric on the bias 5cm (2in) wide and sew it into a tube using the sewing machine. Leave a 0.5cm (¼in) seam allowance. Turn through using a safety pin (see page 14) and stuff using small, even amounts of toy filling.

3 The lightly stuffed tube shown alongside an unstuffed version, made using a slightly narrower tube of fabric. The seam allowance of the latter was trimmed back before turning through, and the tube was then knotted at both ends.

Making cream swirls

These are used to decorate the surface of the cake or candy. They are smaller and less bulky than a cream filling, and are made by stitching down the centre of a length of ribbon and gathering it up. Use a thread that matches the ribbon colour.

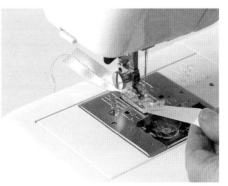 

1 Cut a length of 15mm (¾in) ribbon to the required length and machine stitch along the centre using a long stitch. Do not secure the threads.

2 Take hold of one thread and pull gently, allowing gathers to form in the ribbon at both ends.

Making a cake with conical sides

This method is suitable for larger cakes. The templates are provided on page 62. Begin by cutting out three pieces of fabric for the sides, base and top of the cake. Fold the side piece into a cone shape, right sides together, and stitch the seam on the sewing machine with a 0.5cm (¼in) seam allowance.

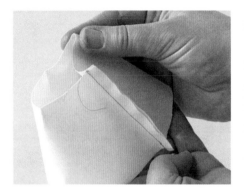

1 Pinch the fabric opposite the seam at the narrow end, and halfway around the rim on either side. Repeat at the wide end of the cone.

2 Pinch the small circle (the cone base) into quarters and pin it to the narrow end of the cone, aligning the marks. Tack the base in position.

3 Machine stitch the base to the cone with a 0.5cm (¼in) seam allowance. Remove the tacking stitches.

4 Attach the top of the cone in the same way, then snip through the side seam to create a 2.5cm (1in) gap for turning through and stuffing.

5 Turn the cone right side out. Tease out the stuffing and, using a pair of scissors, push it into the cone through the gap. When the cone is firmly stuffed, stitch up the gap in the seam by hand.

6 Decorate the cone however you wish. Here, I have created a delicious butterfly cake (see pages 56–57).

Bonded appliqué

This is a great way of attaching fabric shapes to your design. Stars, hearts, flowers and numbers can all be added by following this simple method.

1 Cut a piece of fabric large enough for your chosen shape, and a piece of adhesive web (Bondaweb) the same size. Iron the adhesive web to the wrong side of the fabric, sticky side down.

2 Draw your shape on to the paper backing of the adhesive web, either by hand or using a template, and cut it out.

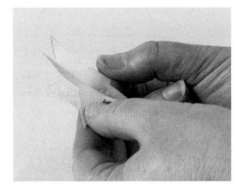

3 Peel the paper backing off the adhesive web.

4 Position the appliqué shape on your fabric, sticky side down, and iron it in place using a hot iron.

5 Stitch around the edge of the shape using machine satin stitch.

Making a basic tart shape

Tarts are a delight to make and come in all sorts of varieties – lemon tarts, fruit tarts, chocolate tarts – simply change the colour of the fabric used for the filling and decorate with your choice of embellishments. Begin by cutting out:

- ♥ two circles of diameter 13cm (5in) – one in beige fabric for the base of the tart and one in coloured fabric for the filling
- ♥ two strips of beige fabric – one 38 x 4cm (15 x 1½in) and one cut on the bias 40.5 x 4cm (16 x 1½in)
- ♥ a strip of iron-on interfacing – 38 x 4cm (15 x 1½in)

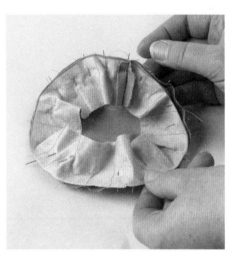

1 Cut out all the pieces as detailed above and attach the iron-on interfacing to the back of the 38cm (15in) strip of fabric.

2 Machine stitch parallel lines of straight stitching at 1cm (½in) intervals across the width of the 38cm (15in) strip.

3 Join the strip into a ring with right sides facing using a 0.5cm (¼in) seam allowance. Mark by pinching the quarter marks on the base of the tart and the ring. Place the ring on the base, right sides together, matching up the quarter marks. Pin then machine stitch the ring in place on the base.

To make the fruit

4 Turn the tart in the right way and pin the topping on the top, with the right side facing you.

5 Tack the topping in position, then pin on the bias strip, with right sides together, as shown in the photograph above.

For a strawberry, make a tiny basic cake shape using a 30mm (1¼in) yo-yo maker or a 7.5cm (3in) diameter circular paper template, then embroider the green leaves using lazy daisy stitch and sew on a sprinkling of seed beads. For the cherry, simply sew a tiny green cross to the top.

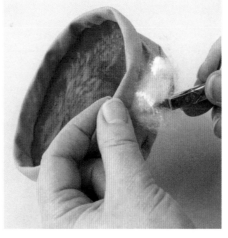

6 Machine stitch around the top of the tart to secure the topping and the pastry edging. Fold the edging over the side of the tart, tuck under the raw edge and pin then hand stitch it in place. This forms the crust that stands up around the outside of the tart.

7 Open up part of the side seam of the tart and stuff with small clumps of stuffing using a pair of scissors.

To make a blackberry, wind up a tiny ball of thick black yarn and stitch through the ball to secure. Then simply cover it with tiny (4mm) black beads.

Projects

Yo-yo maker and equivalent circle template sizes

Large cupcake:
♥ 90mm (3½in) yo-yo maker or 20cm (7¾in) diameter paper circle template

Small cupcake:
♥ 60mm (2¼in) yo-yo maker or 14cm (5½in) diameter paper circle template

Candies and chocolates:
♥ 45mm (1¾in) yo-yo maker or 10cm (4in) diameter paper circle template

On the following pages are twenty projects for different styles of cakes, candies, pies and chocolates – all equally tempting and full of gorgeous ingredients! When you have chosen which project you'd like to make, start by gathering together all of the materials and tools listed at the start of the project. Don't be afraid to vary these if you want to alter the look of your cake or candy – use a different coloured fabric to change the flavour, for example, or beads instead of buttons to change the topping. Most of the projects include one or two variations based on the same techniques – just use your imagination and you will be amazed by the fantastic results you can achieve.

In addition to the tools listed you will require a sewing machine and a basic sewing kit consisting of:

♥ scissors (fabric scissors and embroidery scissors)
♥ pins
♥ sewing needles (see page 10)
♥ machine threads and hand-sewing threads to match the fabric
♥ tape measure
♥ thimble (optional)

All of the basic techniques needed for the projects have been covered in the preceding pages, and you should familiarise yourself with these before starting. Each project is accompanied by step-by-step instructions and photographs of the main stages. Any templates that are required are provided at the back of the book. It is advisable to photocopy or trace these on to paper or card and cut them out before starting the project. Circle templates are not provided as these can easily be drawn on to paper or card using a pair of compasses and a pencil, or by drawing around a plate or lid of the correct size.

Diagrams of all the embroidery stitches used in the projects are provided on page 64.

The instructions for making these colourful cupcakes are provided on pages 46–47.

Sweet Romance

Materials

- ♥ pink silicone cupcake case, 4cm (1½in) across the base
- ♥ pale pink cotton fabric, 21cm (8¼in) square
- ♥ metallic silver fabric for appliqué, 10cm (4in) square
- ♥ silver-lined crystal beads
- ♥ light pink satin ribbon of width 1.5cm (¾in), 2 lengths 66cm (26in) long
- ♥ cream organza ribbon of width 1.5cm (¾in), 66cm (26in) long
- ♥ adhesive web (Bondaweb), 10cm (4in) square
- ♥ toy stuffing
- ♥ metallic silver machine thread

Tools

- ♥ 90mm (3½in) yo-yo maker or 20cm (7¾in) diameter paper circle template
- ♥ beading needle
- ♥ star template (see page 63)

1 Following the instructions for bonded appliqué on page 17, cut out and bond the silver star in the centre of the pink fabric.

2 Machine satin stitch around the edges of the star using metallic silver machine thread.

3 Make the basic cake shape using either the yo-yo maker or a circular paper template (see pages 12–13). If using a yo-yo maker, make sure the star is placed centrally so that it is visible through the hole in the tray part of the yo-yo maker. Carefully stuff the finished cake shape with toy stuffing. The shape is now ready to decorate.

4 To make the cream swirls, gather the three pieces of ribbon to the required length, as described on page 15.

5 Place them in position on the cake and pin along the centre, adjusting the gathers. The organza ribbon forms the lower row, with the two rows of satin ribbon above. Turn under 1.5cm (¾in) at both ends of each length of ribbon and use the gathering threads at each end of the ribbon to sew them in place by hand with a running stitch worked along the centre of the ribbon.

6 Hand sew crystal beads along each edge of the star using sewing cotton and a beading needle.

For the alternative cake, use the small heart template on page 63.

Golden Days

Materials

- ♥ cream silicone cupcake case, 4cm (1½in) across the base
- ♥ cream-coloured cotton fabric, 23 x 13cm (9 x 5in)
- ♥ gold-coloured cotton fabric, 23 x 13cm (9 x 5in)
- ♥ decorative silk rose
- ♥ sparkly heart-shaped button
- ♥ gold-coloured ric-rac braid, 28cm (11in) long
- ♥ organza ribbon of width 1.5cm (¾in), 1 length 66cm (26in) long and 2 lengths 36cm (14¼in) long
- ♥ satin double-sided ribbon of width 1.5cm (¾in), 66cm (26in) long
- ♥ white cotton fabric, 30 x 13cm (11¾ x 5in)
- ♥ cream print cotton fabric, 30 x 13cm (11¾ x 5in)
- ♥ adhesive web (Bondaweb), 30 x 13cm (11¾ x 5in)
- ♥ toy stuffing

Tools

- ♥ 90mm (3½in) yo-yo maker or 20cm (7¾in) diameter paper circle template
- ♥ cake wrap template (page 63)

1 Machine stitch the cream- and gold-coloured fabrics together along their longer edge with a 0.5cm (¼in) seam allowance. Press.

2 Make the basic cake shape using either the yo-yo maker or a circular paper template (see pages 12–13). Ensure the seam is positioned centrally. Carefully stuff the finished cake shape with toy stuffing.

3 Make a cake wrap with the cream print on the right side and plain white fabric on the reverse. Begin by ironing the adhesive web on to the back of the white fabric, sticky side down, then peel off the paper backing and lay the cream print fabric on top, right side facing up. Iron the two together, then draw round the template provided and cut out. Stitch up the seam, turn in the right way and place the silicone cupcake case inside to give it form and rigidity.

4 To make the cream swirls, gather the satin ribbon (see page 15) to the required length and turn under 1.5cm (¾in) at both ends. Hand sew it around the cake using long running stitches, starting and finishing at the seam. Use the gathering threads at either end of the ribbon. Pin then hand stitch a line of ric-rac braid just above the ribbon.

5 Gather the longer length of organza ribbon and hand sew it around the cake wrap, adjusting the gathers as you go. Sew the heart-shaped button on top of the cake. Make a double bow of the shorter lengths of organza ribbon and tie it to the rose stem. Hand sew it in place on the gold side of the cake top. Place the cake in the cake case to finish.

The pretty pink and white cake has been made in the same way using pink and white fabric joined to create four squares. Gathered organza ribbon has been stitched along the seams and one quarter filled with various beads in creams, pinks and purples.

Easter Treats

Materials

- light yellow cotton fabric, 21cm (8¼in) square
- pale blue cotton fabric, 5 x 7.5cm (2 x 3in)
- adhesive web (Bondaweb), 5 x 7.5cm (2 x 3in)
- light green stranded embroidery thread
- light yellow satin ribbon of width 1.5cm (¾in), 2 lengths 66cm (26in) long
- pale blue silicone cupcake case, 4cm (1½in) across the base
- 5 pink and 5 purple 4mm beads
- toy stuffing

Tools

- 90mm (3½in) yo-yo maker or 20cm (7¾in) diameter paper circle template
- egg template (see page 63)

1 Following the instructions for bonded appliqué on page 17, cut out and bond a pale blue egg in the centre of the yellow fabric. Machine satin stitch around the egg using pale blue thread.

2 Machine stitch satin stitch lines across the egg, as shown in the photograph, in yellow and green thread.

3 Embroider by hand a line of running stitches around the outside of the egg, and four lines going across it.

4 Make the basic cake shape using either the yo-yo maker or a circular paper template (see pages 12–13). If using a yo-yo maker, make sure the egg is placed centrally so that it is visible through the hole in the tray part of the yo-yo maker. Carefully stuff the finished cake shape with toy stuffing. The shape is now ready to decorate.

5 To make cream swirls, gather the two pieces of yellow satin ribbon to the required length, as described on page 15. Place them in position on the cake, one above the other, and pin along the centre, adjusting the gathers. Turn under 1.5cm (¾in) at both ends of each length of ribbon and use the gathering threads to sew them in place by hand. Use a running stitch worked along the centre of the ribbon.

6 Hand sew two rows of pink and purple beads on the egg using sewing cotton and a beading needle.

7 Place the cake in the silicone base to finish.

The smaller cake has been made with two different-coloured fabrics joined together and hand embroidered on the top.

Festive Cakes

Materials

- red silicone cupcake case, 4cm (1½in) across the base
- white cotton fabric, 21cm (8¼in) square
- gold-coloured fabric, 6 x 7.5cm (2¼ x 3in)
- adhesive web (Bondaweb), 6 x 7.5cm (2¼ x 3in)
- cream satin ribbon of width 1.5cm (¾in), 66cm (26in) long
- green satin ribbon of width 1.5cm (¾in), 66cm (26in) long
- cream organza ribbon of width 1.5cm (¾in), 1 piece 66cm (26in) long and 1 piece 50cm (20in) long
- toy stuffing
- gold metallic machine thread

Tools

- 90mm (3½in) yo-yo maker or 20cm (7¾in) diameter paper circle template
- beading needle
- bells template (see page 63)

1 Following the instructions for bonded appliqué on page 17, cut out and bond the two gold bells in the centre of the white fabric. Machine satin stitch around the edges of the bells using gold metallic machine thread.

2 Make the basic cake shape using either the yo-yo maker or a circular paper template (see pages 12–13). If using a yo-yo maker, make sure the bells are positioned centrally. Carefully stuff the finished cake shape with toy stuffing. The shape is now ready to decorate.

3 Gather the four pieces of ribbon to the required length, as described on page 15. Place them in position on the cake, one above the other starting with the shorter length of organza at the bottom (make sure this will sit just above the rim of the silicone case), followed by the cream, then the green and finishing with the longer length of organza ribbon at the top. Pin along the centre, adjusting the gathers if necessary. Turn under 1.5cm (¾in) at both ends of each length of ribbon and use the gathering threads to hand sew them in place. Use a running stitch worked along the centre of the ribbon.

4 Place the finished cake in the silicone base to finish.

The Christmas tree template is provided on page 63. For the smaller cake, I have stitched ric-rac braid across the middle of the cake and sewn a button in each quarter.

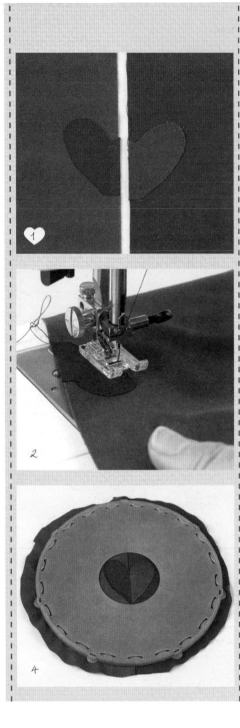

My Valentine

Materials

- ♥ red silicone cupcake case, 4cm (1½in) across the base
- ♥ red cotton fabric, 23 x 13cm (9 x 5in)
- ♥ brown cotton fabric, 23 x 13cm (9 x 5in)
- ♥ brown and red cotton fabric, each 4 x 7cm (1½ x 2¾in)
- ♥ adhesive web (Bondaweb), 4 x 7cm (1½ x 2¾in)
- ♥ brown satin ribbon of width 1.5cm (¾in), 2 lengths 66cm (26in) long
- ♥ toy stuffing

Tools

- ♥ 90mm (3½in) yo-yo maker or 20cm (7¾in) diameter paper circle template
- ♥ half-heart template (see page 63)

1 Cut out two half hearts from the smaller pieces of fabric, one red and one brown. Following the instructions for bonded appliqué on page 17, bond the red half heart to the brown fabric and the brown half heart to the red fabric. Align the edge of each half heart with the longer edges of the fabric.

2 Machine satin stitch around the edges of each half heart using matching thread. Leave the straight edge unstitched.

3 Join the two fabrics together using the sewing machine so that the two halves of the heart match exactly.

4 Make the basic cake shape using either the yo-yo maker or a circular paper template (see pages 12–13). If using a yo-yo maker, make sure the heart is positioned in the middle of the hole in the tray. Carefully stuff the finished cake shape with toy stuffing. The shape is now ready to decorate.

5 Gather the two pieces of brown satin ribbon to the required length, as described on page 15. Place them in position on the cake, one above the other, and pin along the centre, adjusting the gathers. Turn under 1.5cm (¾in) at both ends of each length of ribbon and use the gathering threads to sew them in place by hand. Use a running stitch worked along the centre of the ribbon.

6 Place the cake in a red silicone base to finish.

The small heart template for the smaller cake can be found on page 63.

Pink Candies

Materials

- pink cotton fabric, 8 x 13cm (3¼ x 5in) for each candy
- white cotton fabric, 8 x 13cm (3¼ x 5in) for each candy
- seed beads in variety of pastel colours
- pastel-coloured paper petit four cases
- toy stuffing

Tools

- 45mm (1¾in) yo-yo maker or 10cm (4in) diameter paper circle template
- beading needle

1 Machine stitch the pink and white cotton fabrics together along their longer edge with a 0.5cm (¼in) seam allowance. Press.

2 Make the basic candy shape using either the yo-yo maker or a circular paper template (see pages 12–13). Ensure the seam is positioned centrally. Carefully stuff the finished candy shape with toy stuffing.

3 Sew a dense sprinkling of seed beads on the top and a few more widely spaced on the sides. Use sewing cotton and a beading needle to attach the beads.

4 Place the finished candies in petit four cases.

These lovely little candies make pretty table decorations for weddings and christenings. Make one for each of your guests to take home as a keepsake.

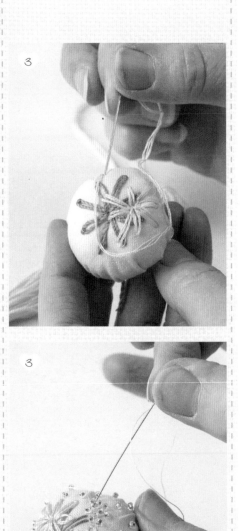

Jewelled Candies

Materials

- ♥ lilac and pink fabric, 13cm (5in) square for each candy
- ♥ silver and lilac seed beads and silver-lined white beads
- ♥ lilac, pink, salmon and pale green stranded embroidery thread
- ♥ toy stuffing
- ♥ paper petit four cases

Tools

- ♥ 45mm (1¾in) yo-yo maker or 10cm (4in) diameter paper circle template
- ♥ beading needle

1 Make the basic candy shape using either the yo-yo maker or a circular paper template (see pages 12–13). Carefully stuff the finished candy shape with toy stuffing.

2 For the heart design, outline a heart shape in two or three lines of running stitch, then add French knots and lilac beads.

3 For the flower designs, either embroider overlapping lazy daisy flowers on top of the candy using pink and salmon-coloured embroidery thread and add clusters of silver beads, or embroider a single lazy daisy flower on top in lilac with leaves in between the petals worked in pale green and sew on silver beads to finish. Attach the beads using sewing cotton and a beading needle.

4 Make as many candies as you wish and place them in petit four cases.

Sugar Shimmers

Materials

- white cotton fabric, 13cm (5in) square for each candy
- crystal sheer fabric, 13cm (5in) square for each candy
- seed pearls
- silver and gold beads
- pink and pale blue crystals
- toy stuffing
- silver and gold foil petit four cases
- pink and pale blue paper petit four cases

Tools

- 45mm (1¾in) yo-yo maker or 10cm (4in) diameter paper circle template
- beading needle

1 Place the crystal sheer fabric on top of the white cotton fabric. Make the basic candy shape with both fabrics together using either the yo-yo maker or a circular paper template (see pages 12–13).

2 Carefully stuff the finished candy shape with toy stuffing.

3 Sew a variety of beads on the top of each candy in a random pattern. Use sewing cotton and a beading needle. I have used silver, pearl and blue beads on some of my candies and pink and gold on the rest.

4 Line each silver and gold petit four case with a pink or pale blue petit four case, and place the candies in these cases. Match the colours to the beads you have used to decorate the candies. I have used a silver petit four case lined with a blue paper case for the candies decorated with silver, pearl and blue beads, and a gold case lined with pink for the pink and gold candies.

These delightful candies make perfect wedding favours. Use colours to match your wedding theme and place one on each place setting at the reception.

Bedazzled

Materials

- brown cotton fabric, 13cm (5in) square for each candy
- toy stuffing
- various red, green and gold seed beads, silver lined and with a metallic finish
- various bugle beads in matching colours
- orange and green stranded embroidery thread
- brightly patterned foil petit four cases
- paper petit four cases in bright colours

Tools

- 45mm (1¾in) yo-yo maker or 10cm (4in) diameter paper circle template
- beading needle

1 Make the basic candy shape using either the yo-yo maker or a circular paper template (see pages 12–13).

2 Carefully stuff the finished candy shape with toy stuffing.

3 Using either lazy daisy stitch or long straight stitch, embroider around the top of each candy in a starburst pattern using either orange or green thread.

4 Sew a variety of beads on the top of each candy using sewing thread and a beading needle. Try placing a small cluster of seed beads on the top, with bugle beads arranged around them. Place the beads in between the embroidery stitches. Sprinkle more seed beads randomly around the sides of each candy.

5 Line each foil petit four case with a paper petit four case, and place the candies inside these. Try out different colour combination until you are happy with the result.

Make these pretty little candies to decorate your table at a fireworks party or Halloween.

Lemon Bonbons

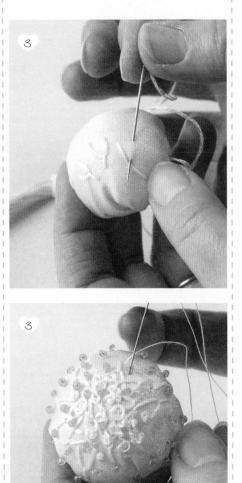

Materials

- yellow cotton fabric, 13cm (5in) square for each candy
- crystal sheer fabric, 13cm (5in) square for each candy
- yellow and crystal beads
- yellow stranded embroidery thread
- toy stuffing
- yellow paper petit four cases

Tools

- 45mm (1¾in) yo-yo maker or 10cm (4in) diameter paper circle template
- beading needle

1 Place the crystal sheer fabric on top of the yellow cotton fabric. Make the basic candy shape with both fabrics together using either the yo-yo maker or a circular paper template (see pages 12–13).

2 Carefully stuff the finished candy shape with toy stuffing.

3 Make as many lemon bonbons as you wish and decorate them with embroidery stitches and beads. Attach the beads using sewing cotton and a beading needle. I have used fly stitch and loose French knots on some of the candies, and only beads on others. Use just two or three strands of the embroidery thread for a delicate look.

4 Place the candies in two petit four cases placed one inside the other.

These tasty bonbons work well in other colours too – try pink for raspberry bonbons or brown for chocolate truffles.

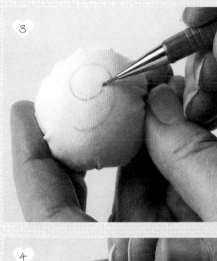

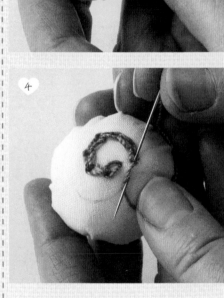

Happy Birthday

Materials

- coloured cotton fabric, 13cm (5in) square for each candy
- various beads in a range of colours and styles, including seed beads and bugle beads
- coloured stranded embroidery thread
- toy stuffing
- paper petit four cases in various colours

Tools

- 45mm (1¾in) yo-yo maker or 10cm (4in) diameter paper circle template
- beading needle
- pencil

1 Make the basic candy shape using either the yo-yo maker or a circular paper template (see pages 12–13).

2 Carefully stuff the finished candy shape with toy stuffing.

3 Make as many candies as you wish in a variety of colours. Draw the age of the child on top of each candy using a pencil.

4 Embroider the number in chain stitch using a thread colour that contrasts with the fabric. For a chunky look, use all six strands of the stranded cotton.

5 Decorate the candies with a variety of beads placed randomly in between the stitching. Attach them using sewing cotton and a beading needle.

6 Place the candies inside two petit four cases placed one inside the other.

Try embroidering on letters of the alphabet to spell out a child's name, or make one for each guest with their own initial on top to take home with them. These colourful candies also make unusual table decorations at anniversary parties. For a house-warming party, embroider on your new house number and hand one to each of your guests as they leave.

Chocolate Box

Materials

- light brown, dark brown and cream cotton fabric, 13cm (5in) square for each chocolate
- pink, cream and brown stranded cotton embroidery thread
- seed beads in a variety of pastel shades
- pearls and pastel-coloured beads
- petit four cases

Tools

- 45mm (1¾in) yo-yo maker or 10cm (4in) diameter paper circle template
- beading needle

1 Make the basic candy shape using either the yo-yo maker or a circular paper template (see pages 12–13). Carefully stuff the finished candy shape with toy stuffing. Make as many chocolates as you wish in a variety of colours.

2 Use contrasting coloured embroidery thread and beads to create the designs on the top of the chocolates. The stranded cotton can be used with all six strands for a chunky look, or split into three strands for a finer thread. The beads are attached with sewing cotton and a beading needle. Use the photographs for reference or make up designs of your own.

3 Place the chocolates in individual petit four cases to finish.

These chocolates look gorgeous presented in a pretty box tied up with ribbon. Real chocolate boxes also work well and make a fun gift for family and friends (of course, you'll have to eat all the real chocolates first!).

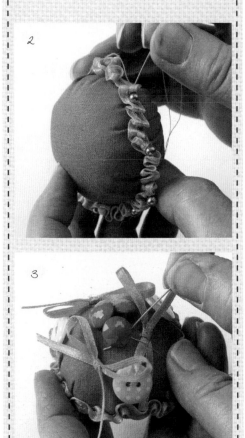

Button Cakes

Materials

For a large cupcake:
- ♥ brightly coloured cotton fabric, 21cm (8¼in) square
- ♥ toy stuffing
- ♥ satin ribbon of width 1.5cm (¾in), 2 lengths 66cm (26in) long
- ♥ narrow satin ribbon of width 6mm (¼in), 23cm (9in) per bow
- ♥ various brightly coloured buttons in different shapes and sizes
- ♥ brightly coloured silicone cupcake case, 4cm (1½in) across the base

For a small cupcake:
- ♥ brightly coloured cotton fabric, 15cm (6in) square
- ♥ toy stuffing
- ♥ narrow satin ribbon of width 6mm (¼in), 1 or 2 lengths 46cm (18in) long
- ♥ narrow satin ribbon of width 2mm (⅛in), 23cm (9in) per bow
- ♥ various brightly coloured buttons in different shapes and sizes
- ♥ brightly coloured silicone cupcake case, 3cm (1¼in) across the base

Tools
- ♥ 90mm (3½in) yo-yo maker or 20cm (7¾in) diameter paper circle template for a large cake, or 60mm (2¼in) yo-yo maker or 14cm (5½in) diameter paper circle template for a small cake

1 Make the basic cake shape using either the yo-yo maker or a circular paper template (see pages 12–13). Carefully stuff the finished cake shape with toy stuffing.

2 Gather one or two pieces of satin ribbon to the required length, as described on page 15. Place the ribbon in position on the cake (one above the other if using two) and pin along the centre, adjusting the gathers. Turn under 1.5cm (¾in) at both ends of each length of ribbon and use the gathering threads to sew them in place by hand. Use a running stitch worked along the centre of the ribbon.

3 Tie the short lengths of narrow ribbon into bows. Use these, along with the buttons, to decorate the top of the cake. Use the photographs as guidance.

4 Place the cake in a silicone cupcake case to finish.

Try adding some simple embroidery to the top of your cakes using six strands of six-stranded cotton, and sew on the buttons in a contrasting thread to introduce even more colour.

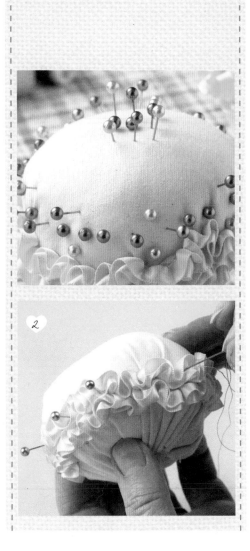

Pincushions

Materials

- white cotton fabric, 21cm (8¼in) square
- toy stuffing
- yellow satin ribbon of width 1.5cm (¾in), 2 lengths 66cm (26in) long
- pins with coloured pearl heads
- thimble
- yellow silicone cupcake case, 4cm (1½in) across the base

Tools

- 90mm (3½in) yo-yo maker or 20cm (7¾in) diameter paper circle template

1 Make the basic cake shape using either the yo-yo maker or a circular paper template (see pages 12–13). Carefully stuff the finished cake shape with toy stuffing.

2 To make cream swirls, gather the two pieces of satin ribbon to the required length, as described on page 15. Place the ribbons in position on the cake, one above the other, and pin along the centre, adjusting the gathers. Turn under 1.5cm (¾in) at both ends of each length of ribbon and use the gathering threads to sew them in place by hand. Use a running stitch worked along the centre of the ribbon.

3 Place the thimble in the cupcake case and sit the cake on top of it. Decorate the top of the cake with pins.

Anyone who enjoys sewing will be delighted by this unique gift – it is not only a pincushion, but a safe place to store your thimble too! Try adding embroidery to the top, perhaps in the form of the recipient's initials or favourite flower, or sew on some tiny beads or buttons.

Meringues

Materials

- coffee-coloured polyester fabric, 51 x 26cm (20 x 10¼in)
- cream polyester fabric, 2 pieces each 8 x 50cm (3¼ x 20in)
- cream polyester fabric, 25 x 13cm (9¾ x 5in)
- brown satin ribbon of width 1cm (½in), 2 lengths 46cm (18in) long
- brown cotton fabric, 7.5cm (3in) square
- toy stuffing

Tools

- 45mm (1¾in) yo-yo maker or 10cm (4in) diameter paper circle template
- 30mm (1¼in) yo-yo maker or 7.5cm (3in) diameter paper circle template
- 23cm (9in) diameter paper circle template

1 Use the 23cm (9in) circle template to cut two circles of coffee-coloured polyester fabric. Follow the instructions on pages 12–13 to make two basic cake shapes. Stuff each one lightly (too much stuffing will make the cake difficult to manage).

2 Place the two cake shapes together with the bases facing and stitch them together about a quarter of the way round.

3 Take the two strips of cream polyester fabric and follow the instructions for making a thick, creamy, piped filling (see page 14). Pull up the gathers until each strip of fabric measures 23cm (9in).

4 Fold over each piece of gathered fabric to make four layers and oversew them together along the stitched edge. Pin and hand sew them to each half of the meringue, about 2.5cm (1in) away from the centre, using running stitch. Make sure that the raw edges are turned under.

5 To make cream swirls, gather the two pieces of brown satin ribbon to the required length, as described on page 15. Place a gathered ribbon on the outer edge of the cream filling, pin and hand sew it in place. Repeat on the other side of the meringue. Remember to turn under both ends of each ribbon for a neat finish.

6 Make a small, chocolate ball using either the 30mm (1¼in) yo-yo maker or the 7.5cm (3in) circle template (see pages 12–13) and stuff it firmly. Attach it within the folds of cream.

7 Make two rosettes from cream fabric using the 45mm (1¾in) yo-yo maker or the 10cm (4in) circle template (see pages 12–13). Sew one to each side of the meringue to neaten the edges and help hold the cake together.

Change the colour scheme to white, cream and red for a delicious-looking fruit meringue.

Tea-time Treats

Materials

- white cotton fabric, 28 x 23cm (11 x 9in)
- white satin ribbon of width 1.5cm (¾in), 1 length 92cm (36¼in) long, 1 length 61cm (24in) long and 1 length 46cm (18in) long
- white organza ribbon of width 1.5cm (¾in), 2 lengths 61cm (24in) long
- sparkly white cotton fabric, 7.5cm (3in) square for each frosted berry
- silver-lined glass seed beads
- pale pink stranded embroidery thread
- toy stuffing

Tools

- 30mm (1¼in) yo-yo maker or 7.5cm (3in) diameter paper circle template
- beading needle
- conical cake templates (see page 62)

1 Make the basic cake shape following the instructions on page 16. Stuff the cake firmly.

2 To make cream swirls, gather all the satin and organza ribbons as described on page 15. Hand sew the 61cm (24in) satin ribbon around the top of the cake using running stitch. Use the gathering threads to stitch with and adjust the gathers as you work round the cake. Neaten the ends of the ribbon by tucking them under by 1.5cm (¾in) at both ends.

3 Hand sew the two lengths of organza ribbon around the cake, just below the satin ribbon, following the same method.

4 Start to stitch the 92cm (36¼in) satin ribbon around the top of the cake, next to the first ribbon. Work the ribbon into cream swirls on the top of the cake, leaving a gap in the middle of each swirl for a frosted berry.

5 Make approximately three small, white frosted berries using the sparkly white cotton fabric and either the 30mm (1¼in) yo-yo maker or the 7.5cm (3in) circle template (see pages 12–13). Stuff each ball firmly.

6 Decorate each berry with an embroidered flower worked in lazy daisy stitch using two or three strands of pale pink embroidery thread, and attach a sprinkling of glass seed beads. Attach each berry to the top of the cake, nestling inside the cream swirls.

7 Hand sew the 46cm (18in) length of satin ribbon around the base of the cake, following the method above, to finish.

Chocolate and strawberry versions of this cake look equally delicious.

Fondant Fancies

Materials

- pink cotton fabric, 28 x 23cm (11 x 9in)
- cream-coloured polyester fabric, 3 x 38cm (1¼ x 15in) cut on the bias (see page 15)
- pink satin ribbon of width 2mm (⅛in), 38cm (15in) long
- pink satin ribbon of width 1.5cm (¾in), 1 length 46cm (18in) long and 1 length 61cm (24in) long
- cream-coloured lace of width 2cm (¾in) with one straight edge, 1.2m (48in) long
- pearl beads
- pink seed beads
- toy stuffing

Tools

- beading needle
- conical cake templates (see page 62)

1 Make the basic cake shape following the instructions on page 16. Stuff the cake firmly.

2 To make cream swirls, gather the two lengths of 1.5cm (¾in) satin ribbon (see page 15). Hand sew the 61cm (24in) satin ribbon around the top of the cake using running stitch. Use the gathering threads to stitch with and adjust the gathers as you work round the cake. Neaten the ends of the ribbon by tucking them under by 1.5cm (¾in) at both ends. Sew the shorter length around the base of the cake in the same way.

3 Cut the lace into two pieces. Gather both lengths along the straight side. Sew them to the side of the cake, one under the other, just below the satin ribbon.

4 Attach the seed beads and pearl beads in pairs around the top of the cake. To attach each pair of beads, use a beading needle and thread on one seed bead. Remove the needle and pass both ends of the thread through the eye of the needle. Now thread on one pearl bead and sew the pair of beads to the top of the cake.

5 Make the cream-coloured polyester fabric into a narrow tube, turn through and knot the ends (see page 15). Place it with the narrow pink satin ribbon and tie in a bow.

Make two or three of these lovely cakes for a special friend and present them in a pretty cake tin that they can then use for storing real cakes – perfect for anyone who loves baking!

Butterfly Cakes

Materials

- white cotton fabric, 30 x 30cm (11¾ x 11¾in)
- apricot-coloured satin ribbon of width 1.5cm (¾in), 1 length 46cm (18in) long,
  1 length 61cm (24in) long, 2 lengths 25cm (9¾in) long and 1 length 50cm (20in) long
- cream-coloured satin ribbon of width 1.5cm (¾in), 61cm (24in) long
- white organza ribbon of width 1.5cm (¾in), 66cm (26in) long
- pearl beads
- toy stuffing

Tools

- beading needle
- conical cake and butterfly wing templates (see page 62)

1 Make the basic cake shape following the instructions on page 16. Stuff the cake firmly.

2 Cut out four semi-circles from the white fabric using the butterfly wing template. Stitch them together in pairs, right sides facing, leaving a gap for turning and stuffing. Turn the wings in the right way and stuff firmly. Sew up the gap.

3 Pin each wing in position on the top of the cake, leaving a 2cm (¾in) gap between them. Hand stitch them in place along the straight edge only.

4 To make cream swirls, gather all the satin ribbons (see page 15). Hand sew the 61cm (24in) apricot-coloured satin ribbon around the top of the cake using running stitch. Use the gathering threads to stitch with and adjust the gathers as you work round the cake. Neaten the ends of the ribbon by tucking them under by 1.5cm (¾in) at both ends. Attach the 46cm (18in) apricot-coloured ribbon around the base of the cake in the same way, then attach the cream-coloured ribbon around the top, just below the apricot-coloured ribbon. Work the 50cm (20in) length of apricot-coloured ribbon between the two butterfly wings and the two 25cm (10in) lengths on the outside of the wings.

5 Cut and attach a 30cm (11¾in) length of organza ribbon around the outside of the cake. Make a bow from the remaining piece of organza ribbon and attach it to the side of the cake on top of the first piece. Decorate the top of the cake with a line of pearl beads on either side of the butterfly wings, and add further beads in a line around the organza ribbon.

The chocolate version of this cake looks just as delicious, especially when topped with a red cherry (see page 19 for how to make it).

Fruit Tarts

Materials

- beige cotton fabric, 46 x 56cm (18 x 22in), or a fat quarter
- red cotton fabric, 15cm (6in) square
- iron-on interfacing, 38 x 4cm (15 x 1½in)
- red satin ribbon of width 1.5cm (¾in), 2 lengths 71cm (28in) long
- 7.5cm (3in) squares of purple and red cotton fabric for the strawberries and cherries
- small amount of thick, black yarn for the blackberries
- green stranded embroidery thread
- small (4mm) black beads and red beads
- red seed beads
- toy stuffing

Tools

- 30mm (1¼in) yo-yo maker or 7.5cm (3in) diameter paper circle template
- 13cm (5in) diameter paper circle template
- ruler and pencil
- beading needle

1 Make the tart following the instructions on pages 18–19.

2 To make cream swirls, gather the two lengths of satin ribbon as described on page 15. Hand sew them around the top of the tart using running stitch, one inside the other. Use the gathering threads to stitch with and adjust the gathers as you work around the tart. Neaten the ends of the ribbon by tucking them under by 1.5cm (¾in) at both ends.

3 Make a selection of fruits (see page 19). Arrange them on the top of the tart using a few stitches placed underneath to secure.

The strawberry pavlova in the foreground has been made from cream-coloured fabric and has cream and jam swirls, made from cream-coloured and red satin ribbon, around the outside of the pavlova and on the top. I have added a smooth, cream edging to the top of the pavlova, made from a stuffed tube of fabric cut on the bias (see page 15). The dessert is finished with strawberries sewn on the top.

Alternatively, use a yellow fabric filling to make a lemon tart, and decorate with yellow and cream swirls.

Cherry Turnover

Materials

- cream-coloured cotton fabric, 30 x 15cm (11¾ x 6in)
- thin wadding, 30 x 15cm (11¾ x 6in)
- cream polyester fabric, 8 x 50cm (3¼ x 20in)
- cream satin ribbon of width 1cm (½in), 50cm (20in) long
- red satin ribbon of width 1.5cm (¾in), 50cm (20in) long
- pre-gathered cream lace of width 2.5cm (1in), 50cm (20in) long
- toy stuffing
- red cotton fabric, 7.5cm (3in) square for each cherry

Tools

- 30mm (1¼in) yo-yo maker or 7.5cm (3in) diameter paper circle template
- 13cm (5in) diameter paper circle template

1 Cut two circles of cotton fabric and two of wadding using the 13cm (5in) paper circle template. Assemble the four circles in layers with the two pieces of wadding in the centre and the fabric on the outside, right sides facing outwards. Machine stitch across the centre of the circle first and then machine stitch the fabric and wadding together round the edge, 0.5cm (¼in) from the fabric edge. Do not neaten the edges.

2 Fold the prepared circle in half, pin and sew a line of machine stitches about 2cm (¾in) long and about 2cm (¾in) from the folded edge.

3 To make cream swirls, gather all the ribbons as described on page 15 and pull up the gathers until the length is about 18cm (7in).

4 Attach the gathered ribbons to the upper inside edge of the turnover, cream on the outside and then the red. Hand sew them in place using running stitch and adjust the gathers as you work round the turnover. Tuck the ends neatly inside the cake.

5 Hand sew the gathered lace around the lower edge of the turnover, and around the upper edge just below the red ribbon.

6 Cut the cream polyester fabric into two pieces each 8 x 25cm (3¼ x 10in) and make them into thick, piped cream following the instructions on page 14. Pull up the gathers until each piece measures about 15cm (6in) long. Stuff one length lightly with toy stuffing and leave the other one empty.

7 Hand stitch both tubes to the lower part of the turnover, the empty piece first and the stuffed piece on top. Turn under the raw edges to neaten.

8 Make two cherries using the yo-yo maker or the 7.5cm (3in) diameter paper circle template and hand sew them amongst the cream.

Templates

conical cake base
increase by 50%

butterfly cake wings
increase by 50%

conical cake sides
increase by 50%

conical cake top
increase by 50%

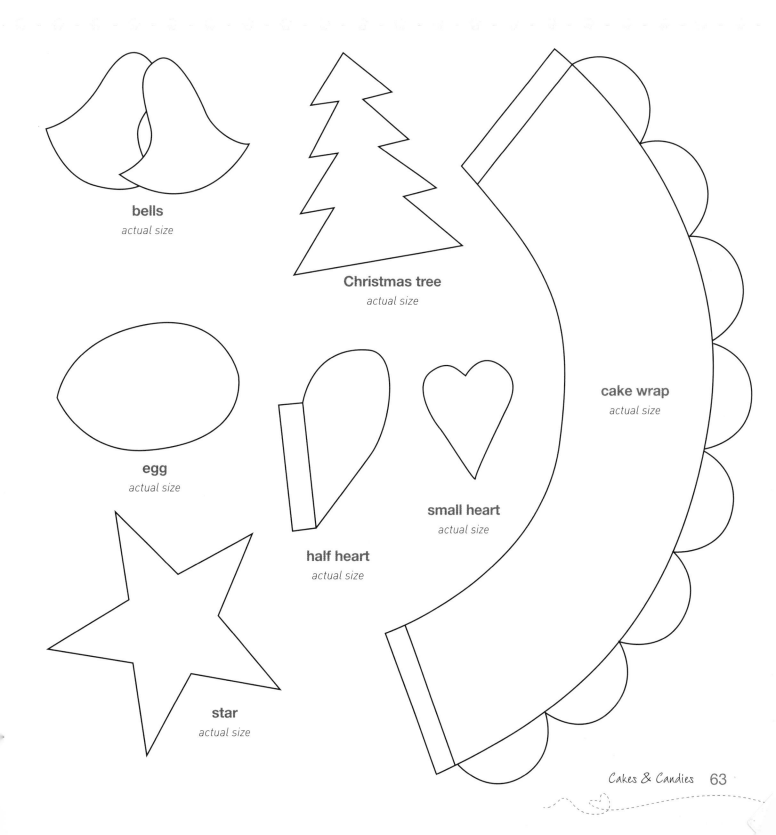

bells
actual size

Christmas tree
actual size

egg
actual size

half heart
actual size

small heart
actual size

cake wrap
actual size

star
actual size

Stitches

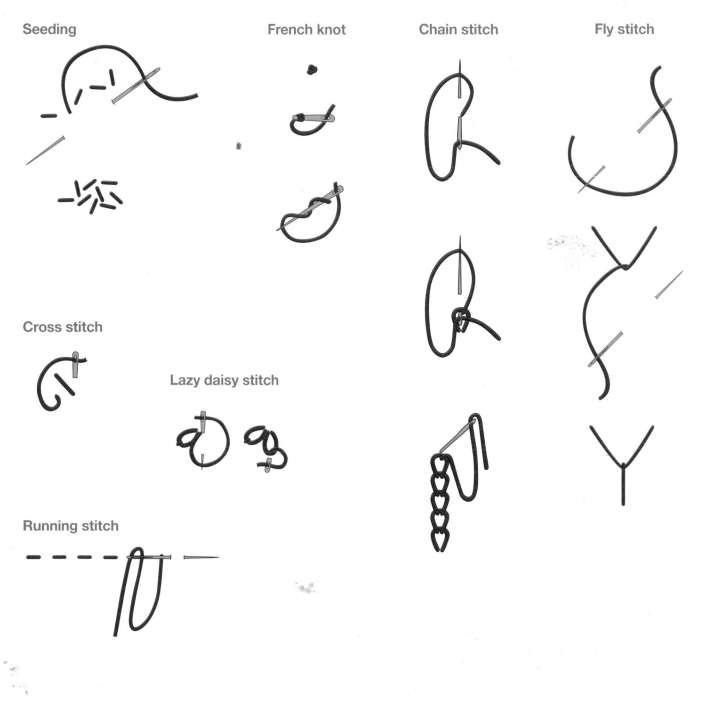

Seeding

French knot

Chain stitch

Fly stitch

Cross stitch

Lazy daisy stitch

Running stitch